# THE
# BEGINNING
# OF THE
# NEVER ENDING

## A Collection Of Poems For The Soul

by
Nigel Barnes

*May your light
internally shine.*

*Nigel Barnes*

# THE
# BEGINNING
# OF THE
# NEVER ENDING

**A Collection Of Poems For The Soul**

by
Nigel Barnes

**Jarrett Press & Publications**
Hillsborough, North Carolina

This book was printed on acid free paper.

Published May 26, 1997

Editing of the original manuscript for this book was performed by Shakara Barnes
Final copy editing and typesetting by William G. Carrington
Original cover art and graphics by Luis Franco




Library of Congress Catalog Card Number: 97-072840
Barnes, Nigel D., 1976-
        The Beginning of the Never Ending

ISBN  1-888701-03-X (paper)




Copies of this book may be obtained from Jarrett Press & Publications, POB 1295, Hillsborough, NC 27278. Quantity order discounts for non profit groups available.

This book is dedicated to the divine light
that shines in us all.

# ACKNOWLEDGMENTS

First and foremost, I would like to thank the Creator.
Mere words cannot express how grateful I am to him
for giving me the insight, pleasure, and ability to love him.

I would also like to thank my parents, family, and friends for their sacrifices,
support, encouragement, and most of all for believing in me when I didn't
even believe in myself. You each hold a very special place in my heart.

Special thanks to Nayya MalachiZodok-EL,
H.T.M. and the A.M.O.M.

# TABLE OF CONTENTS

# ABOUT THE AUTHOR

Nigel Barnes, a lifelong resident of Durham, N.C., is currently a student at North Carolina Central University, majoring in journalism. He has accepted the challenge of carrying the divine torch of righteousness and truth revealed to him in 1994 through his first poem The Prophecy. With his compassion for poetry, as well as his sincere concern for the deteriorating moral climate of today, Nigel continuously awakens the souls of many through poetic readings in schools, churches, radio shows, special events, and individual projects. His captivating poetry is truly a blessing to us all.

# The Prophecy

Everything was dark.
My eyes were closed.
Then I saw a spark,
And a man arose.
"Follow me," he said,
"Hold on to my hand,"
I asked if I was dead,
For I did not understand.
The man gave a smile.
He had a twinkle in his eye.
Curiosity was driving me wild.
So I asked him the reason why-
"Why am I here?
What bad have I done?"
"My son have no fear,
For you are the chosen one."
He said no more,
But on his face was a grin.
Then he opened a door,
That's when I saw the pen.
It was made out of gold,
A true marvel to see.
I shivered not from the cold,
For something had taken over me.
Rapidly beating was my heart beat,
As the man jumped into my soul.
I could no longer stand on my feet.
Of my body I lost total control.

Then it was a voice I heard,
It sounded real odd.
"My child, you are hearing my word,
For I am God.
With paper and pen
You will give the world light.
You will end all sin,
And make everything right.
If there is anything you need
I am only a prayer away.
For you are chosen indeed,
So you must now lead the way."
Was it only a dream?
Was it just my imagination?
But so real it all seems,
Can my words really bring salvation?

At this present time I had no idea what to do or what to say
So I closed my eyes and I began to pray:

Oh, Most High,
Let my mind be the shrine of the divine.
Permeate your word through my spirit.
Stimulate my perception so as I may hear it.
Navigate my thinking as my brain explores.
Consecrate my words as I translate yours.
Allow me to view all things metaphysically.
Introspectively give me no doubt of my potentiality.
Allow my true divinity to completely manifest.
Let my light shine, Oh Lord, and I will do the rest.
Amen.

And when I opened my eyes,
I could feel the divine light being manifested,
Leaving all of my brain tunnels feeling congested,
Like heavy traffic,
Graphic visions of thought collisions,
And word accidents that implement
frequent mental experiments
from segments of my mind that are heaven-sent.
I get consent from over ninety percent of my mind
that the words represent,
Yet, to some extent I find,
there are discontent cells that try to disorient,
But you see,
to me their arguments are irrelevant.
For they could never prevent the event
of me being confident in the content of my material.
Serial numbers are branded
on the imperial thoughts mentally handed
down to me spiritually.
Not even I can see
with my eyes,
I visualize with my soul,
Control of the whole earth,
The birth of cold to heat transforms,
as it warms my mind,
spreading like wild fire,
Words I find embedding the entire
cortex of my brain,

It's almost too complex to explain.
My mental domain contains psychological chains
that strain my membrane
causing migraines,
But yet and still I maintain.
With the strength of hurricanes,
I bring rains that ease the pain
and break the leash,
That's why my powers are increased
once words are released
from my mouth,
To say the least,
Masterpiece.

# The Beginning

## of the

## Never Ending

# Day By Day

Another year has come and gone
Another day has passed,
What new things will my eyes look upon
As I peek into the looking glass?

I have no idea of what lies ahead
I'm just going to take it day by day,
I know in my heart I have nothing to dread
As long as God continues to lead my way.

His path I will always follow
For I know that he knows what is best,
He will never give me more than I can swallow
Or make the burden too heavy on my chest.

I feel blessed everyday when I awaken
And behold another breathtaking sunrise,
I thank the Most High for every breath I have taken
And for allowing his light to always manifest in my eyes.

# A Heavenly Shrine

My eyes have seen the beauty of a heavenly shrine
Magnificent and majestic in every sense.
The way my heart pounded almost blew my mind
For I could truly feel the divine presence.

Then I saw the soul of the shrine open wide
Blessing me with a chance to walk through its door.
I thanked the Most High as I stepped inside
Now my heart shall be alone no more.

# I Dance In The Rain

I dance in the rain,
But my body stays dry.
I feel no pain,
Although hurting am I.

The sun makes me hot,
As its rays sting my eyes,
Although a bird I am not,
I still know I belong in the skies.

I have worked for less than a dollar,
So what have I really achieved?
I once heard Mother Earth holler,
But no help did she receive.

I watch the moon frown.
I watch the sun smile.
But they both saw me drown,
And walk my last mile.

I took a train across the sea.
I caught a whale along the way.
People better stop looking at me,
Before I think them all away.

Powerful is my mind.
Just as shining is my soul.
I journey through dimensions of time,
But I never seem to grow old.

I have walked through the burning pits of Hell,
And with the Devil had a fight.
He looked me in the eyes and told me never to tell
That I beat him up that night.

Some say my thoughts are insane.
They say crazy am I.
But I still dance in the rain,
While my body stays dry.

# Awaken

Awaken my sleeping child
Awaken from the slumbering sleep
that leaves your mind in a dormant state
Awaken from the lethargic coma
that is hindering your divinity to formulate,
Awaken with the innocence of a child
whose mind has not yet been corrupted
Awaken with the exhalation of a volcano
whose lava has recently erupted,

Awaken my sleeping child
Whatever you are presently doing,
you must stop and move with great haste
You have already slept until now,
it is imperative that no more time you waste,
You must release the divine thoughts
that are presently shackled in your mind
Unleash my spirit and we can overcome
all obstacles once we are combined,

Awaken my sleeping child
Your thought is your life.
It always was and it will surely forever be
Just imagine viewing your life
through and with the eyes of me,
You will feel no pain,
your days of sorrow will be long in the past
Your soul will rise to any occasion
and through all negativity stand fast,

Awaken my sleeping child
I have given you the power to think,
I have blessed you with all that you need
You must manifest your thinking as divine,
just as a flower manifests from a seed,
At this present time you are more
than you ever could have hoped or dreamed
But you must consciously know that within you
I live as the Lord Supreme,

Awaken my sleeping child
For I have watched your mind being stagnated
for far too long
I have watched you admit to being weak
when I know I have made you strong,
For you are a part of me
just as a wave is a part of the ocean
Know that I have made you in control
of all your emotions,

Awaken my sleeping child
Awaken for it has been said
that the Kingdom of Heaven is now at hand
But wordly desires will keep you from Heaven's door.
This you must overstand-
You can climb the highest mountain,
and you can search the deepest sea
But the answer that you seek lives right in your soul
for that answer is me.

Awaken!

# Illusions

Disillusioned is man's mind
Look deeper and you will find,
Puzzled is the face of the rejected
Death is the drug they injected,
Power is the cause of the gleam in their eyes
Demonic is the dream in which they all fantasize,
Corrupt is the man who claims he is not
Foolish, for he has sold his soul for all he has got,
Periodically time in the psychological sense stands still
Unfortunately the sleeping mind cannot distinguish the real,
For the dream world has many a trick up its sleeve
Not for all to know, only the chosen do believe,
For deaf are your ears, Just as blind are your eyes
Transparent are your fears, Which all do realize,
The loser is the man who can never win
The winner is the man who has just won,
The suicidal think to live life is a sin
The souls light will shine bright like the sun,
To swim in deep waters is to drown out at sea
To see clearly through the illusions you must believe in me,
When I say me, I am really referring to you
The one with all the questions wondering what you should do,
To find the answers you must channel your mind with the deep
Focus your soul on reality and you will soon
Awaken from your sleep.

# I Have No Reason To Worry

The sun's heat freezes my body
The sound of the thunder hurts my eyes
Mother Earth's teardrops have flooded my land
But yet and still I rise

Earthquakes are piecing the land together
Wind blew away my legs, so I walk on my hands
The melting snow keeps my body warm at night
But yet and still I stand

Through all the heartache and pain
Through all the stress  and the strife
I know that I will come out alright
For I have given the Lord- my life

Although the clouds have covered the sky
Although the world is about to end
Although I don't believe I want to die
I can't wait to live with the Lord my friend

# My Journey Home

Deep in the valley of darkness,
I realize that I am blind,
I stumble trying to get out,
But no escape do I find.
I have no idea where I've been,
Nor do I know where I will end.
All I know is that I am lost,
Confused and without a friend.
If only I had a guide,
Maybe they could help see me through.
But there is nobody out here but me.
Oh, What am I to do?
Then I felt a strange sensation,
Of magnitude I cannot explain.
My body started to tremble,
As my spirit became drained.
It scared me so much
That I soon began to weep.
Exhaustion took over my body,
And I cried myself slowly to sleep.
My mind began to wander,
As my life turned into a dream.
I heard a powerful voice inside my head.
It was the voice of the Lord Supreme.

He said he has always been with me.
But I had never paid attention.
He said for all my sins I will be forgiven,
If I follow one simple condition.
I asked what it was,
Just tell me and it will be done.
"Cleanse your soul," he said
"And with me you will become one.
You said you wanted a guide,
Then you need to follow my path.
You must free your mind,
And with my spirit take a bath.
I know that change is not easy
So I will give you a moment to decide."
I said, "I choose to be with you."
Then the doors to the divine light opened wide.
I felt excruciating pain
Every part of my body was sore.
Then I heard a voice in my head,
Saying that I would feel pain no more.
"My child wherever you are,
You will always be with me,
Your world will be no longer dark
For I have given you a light in which all will see,
As you awaken from your sleep
Everything you will understand,
Your eyes will open, you will see the light
And with me you will forever stand."

# Transitions

Focus your attention on the word transitions.
By no means is this a musical rendition,
but it is a poetically inclined composition.

First of all, to end all suspicion,
I am no wizard or magician,
Although I am known to write magic,
Tragic it may seem,
But my dream keeps me alive,
God tells me I will survive
if I work with a
smile,
and the whole world smiles with you,
because they are happy,
birthday to you,
I thought you knew,
but now I know you know
right from wrong
answer,
next guess please.
Just ease your mind with my words,
For what you thought you heard,
May not be what I am saying
To the Heavens I am praying,
But with your mind I am playing,
A game of mine called "Transitions."

Excuse me as I pause for an intermission,
I want to give everyone who inspired me
the proper recognition,
Although I always had ambition,
It was you who put the key in my mental ignition,
Without you I wouldn't be in this position,
So I say thanks.

Now let's continue with transitions.
Let your mind feed off the transitional expressions,
For they are designed for mental digestion.
I see your mind is still starving,
So my words are gently carving,
A pathway to your brain,
Does that make me insane?
Never,
because I always maintain my sanity,
Pure reality while you wonder
how can it be
true,
cross my heart and hope to die,
Ask me no question I tell you no lie
detector test,
Honestly, I didn't manifest,
O.K. I confess, I did it,
but I had no choice,
only a voice in the matter,
Mad like the hatter,
The voices make me madder,
There's too much chatter in my brain
storming,

I can feel my mind slowly transforming
words into phrase form,
I perform until your soul is left warm,
So inform me when it is blazing,
gazing at the fire you say,
"Amazing"
Grace,
As you praise the Lord,
Looking toward his guiding light,
Guiding you safely through the night-
time is the right time for love,
So I look up above before I close my eyes,
Wise because I have knowledge of self,
Wealth only in the spiritual sense,
But health and infinite wisdom are condensed
into my cerebrum and yours.
Our kingdom is Heaven
only knows what the future holds,
So take it day by day,
Never stray from God's arms where you now safely lay,
Pray when you can,
Overstand God's plan and you will become a better man.
For right now this is all I have to say,
Make sure you come again another day,
For another edition of transitional word play.

# Troubled Waters

Troubled are the waters in which I now swim
Bright was the light that I watch slowly dim,
Distant I feel at times when you I cannot see
I question, "Am I worthy of you believing in me?"

I will continue to try for you said it can be done
I find myself losing a battle I had thought to be won.
I know now I must fight if I want to achieve
And I am ready for war, for in your word I do believe.

# The Drawers Are Open

The drawers are open to my second hand thoughts
My brain is being baked in the stove,
Airplane tickets to Heaven I bought
Into the fiery pits of Hell I dove,

I picked up the phone, No voice did I hear
My watch said it's time to begin,
I am tired of living my life in fear
So I must now bring my life to an end.

# Knocking On Heavens Door

I knock, I knock,
On Heavens door.
There is no answer,
I knock some more.

"Please Oh Lord, Come open the gate!"
"I'm sorry my child, But you chose your fate."

"Please Oh Lord, Just let me in!"
"Remember your past, Remember your sins."

"Please Oh Lord, Just let me explain!"
"You failed to obey my commandments
when they were written very plain."

"Please Oh Lord, I have changed my ways!"
"You knew not my word, So I must turn you away."

I knocked, I knocked on Heavens door.
Now I shall burn in Hell forevermore.

# Divine Victory

If a rose should bloom in the dead of the night,
If the skies should fall from up above,
I have no doubt everything will be alright.
For I have given the Most High my love.

If the moon should shine brighter than the sun,
If all the oceans should turn into sand,
I have no doubt that my war's already won.
For it is with my Creator that I will eternally stand.

# Stormy Winds

Endless are the days,
Even longer are the nights.
Stormy winds leave black haze,
Fogging every souls' sight.

The nurturing whisper of the wind,
Supplying a breeze to the falling leaf,
The waterfall's crashing end
A forgotten soul's never ending grief

A love of two separate hearts
Stagnated by distant miles,
As the strength of one departs
The serpent hides his smiles.

The silent prayer rings loud in the soul
Out of the mist a drop of sunshine will appear.
God will shelter your heart from the cold
Just as he will wipe away your mind's tear.

# My Special Day

Of all my days, I must say today is my best
My soul is finally free and my body has been put to rest.
Today was the day when my eyelids did close
Then my soul left my body and to Heaven it rose.
Today I soared through the sky like I was a bird in flight.
I walked straight through Heaven's gates led by a guiding light.
Today I looked down at Earth and everything I left behind
But if you look inside my heart, nothing but joy will you find.
I have spent many years on Earth, this I must confess.
But out of all of my days, I must say today is my best.

# My Dying Bed

As I lay here on my dying bed,
My life here on earth has come to an end.
Instead of looking back, I am looking ahead,
Waiting for my new life with you to begin.

# We Can

The Creator has blessed the human race
With the ability to do many things.
So why walk around with a sad face
Complaining of all the pain life brings?

For although we are all unique
Special in every conceivable way,
Being different is not what makes us weak
It is how we choose to spend our day.

We become too content with what we do
With no motivation to do anymore.
We have not even the slightest clue
Of what great things life has in store.

We must look deep inside of our hearts
And use the full potential of our minds.
Only then will all the boredom depart
And our true purpose in life will we find.

We must all believe in our souls,
Whether we be woman or man.
No matter what negative things we are told,
We must know deep down inside that we can.

# Life's Riddle

My life is a riddle
A puzzle waiting to be solved,
My body is stuck in the middle
Of the earth as it revolves.

I am granted only so much time
With so many pieces I have yet to put together,
To not succeed would be a crime
And my life would be doomed forever.

Working fast though I am
I still need to pick up the pace,
Sometimes I feel as if I'm damned
When the pieces don't  fit into place.

It's times like this I say to myself
I know I will reach my goal,
And when I take my last breath
My Creator will have my soul.

# How Do I Get To The Kingdom Of Heaven

I had a soul searching dream one night
I was standing in the world all alone
I was on a quest for the divine light
A journey to find the divine throne

I can remember being lost
I did not know where to begin
I felt to fail was to pay the cost
And to find the Kingdom of Heaven was to win

How do I get to the Kingdom of Heaven
I felt that surely the sun would know
So I asked the sun this question-
"Oh, great sun, which way do I go?"

The sun looked at me and said with a smile,
"Your thoughts must be as pure as the water that flows"
So I walked until I reached the great river Nile
I took a sip, but the Kingdom of Heaven still did not show

How do I get to the Kingdom of Heaven
I felt that surely the moon would know
So I asked the moon this question-
"Oh great moon, which way do I go?"

The moon looked down and said with a grin
"You must look deep down at the very core."
I dug until I had reached the earth's origin
But I still could not see heavens door

How do I get to the Kingdom of Heaven
I felt that surely the stars would know
So I asked the stars this question-
"Oh, great stars, which way do I go?"

The stars gazed down and said with a smirk,
"Your mind must be as grand as the skies."
So I climbed the highest mountain with much work
But I still could not see the heavens to my discouraged surprise

There was nobody left to ask
So I dropped to my knees and cried
Instantly I felt the earth start to quake
And the skies burst open wide

A thunderous voice said unto me-
"All that you must do is stand.
You are in the image of my divinity
For the Kingdom of Heaven is now at hand

I have blessed you with a mind to think pure thoughts
I have blessed you with a brain that is grander than the skies
I have blessed you with a soul that is the core of your existence
To see the Kingdom of Heaven just open your eyes."

# At The Top

I have a strong voice,
But my words are seldom heard.
I have keen hearing,
But my ears are subjected to nothing but torture.
I have perfect vision,
But my eyes have yet to see the light.
I have a sharp mind,
But it is almost never challenged.
I am forced to have respect for everyone
When I receive respect from only a few.
I have a strong God,
Culture,
And knowledge of myself,
By having a strong body,
Mind,
And soul,
I know that nothing
And that nobody can bring me down,
Nothing can stop me from rising to the top.
So at the top I shall eternally stand.

# I Walk On The Moon

I walk on the moon, I survived a typhoon, Better stop me soon,
The sky's overcast, My nine I will blast, No man will last.

I cry to myself, My teardrops are filled with blood,
All I see is death, Another body lying in the mud,
Please tell me why, the sun's rays refuse beam,
Tell me why I want to die, But I'm dead already it seems,

I walk on the moon, I survived a typhoon, Better stop me soon,
The sky's overcast, My nine I will blast, No man will last.

Dancing in a volcanic eruption,
Romancing my own mind with corruption,
Pasting my neck on the wire,
Then finally tasting of the eternal fire,

I walk on the moon, I survived a typhoon, Better stop me soon,
The sky's overcast, My nine I will blast, No man will last.

I froze every sea, Just for drowning me,
That's why my mind is about to pop,
I stung a bee, The first time in history,
So will the madness ever stop,
I copped a plea, And got off scott free,
Another bomb I will surely drop,
For I'll shout with glee, Just you wait and see,
When I stand at the top,

I walk on the moon, I survived a typhoon, Better stop me soon,
The sky's overcast, My nine I will blast, No man will last.

# Lightning Don't Strike Me Now

Lightning, don't strike me now

As my body dances in between
The realms of right and wrong
As I fight to keep my mind clean
While I struggle to stay strong

Lightning, don't strike me now

As I walk around with my head hanging down
Crying tears of pain and tears of sorrow
Knowing I should smile but can only manage a frown
Never even looking toward the beauty of tomorrow

Lightning don't strike me now

As I wrestle with thoughts of evil and hate
Lying about emotions that I have and those I do not
Putting on a mask disguising my own heavenly fate
Trying to take all I can, but not using anything I've got

Lightning don't strike me now

Because somehow I can feel the power of the storm
The clouds of death seeming to follow me more and more
But all I need is a little more time for my life to transform
So that when I die, I can walk through those divine doors

Lightning don't strike me!

# The Wisdom In The Word

In the silent darkness of the shadow hour
Suspended stares watch the lunar reflect the light from the sun
Floating bodies of water prepare for a midnight shower
Voices from Heaven sing of how the war will be won

Mother Earth struggles to fight off man's constant attacks
The four winds patiently hold everything in place
The chosen wait for the day when the chariots come back
Gravity causes many to forget they live in outer space

The golden cycle will make many hide underground
For the silver cycle has finally reached its end
Whispers ride with the wind at the speed of sound
Many ears hear, but few have the wisdom to comprehend

Seeds of life are carefully planted in the womb of the earth
Kings and Queens sit majestically on their rightful thrones
Vibrations of this land are felt long before a mother gives birth
And they are felt long after a soul leaves its flesh and bones

The fallen angel often looks up to the stars
The three dimensions become nonexistent in dreams
Our everyday trials make Heaven seem so far
When the divine kingdom is right upon us it seems

Foundations are made even when the eyes may appear closed
Silence is the only sound those who listen ever heard
The world is a stage so everybody strike their pose
But never take for granted the wisdom that lives in the word

# Rainbow Of Hope

My heart was filled with pain
Deep in a depression I was crying,
Tears dropped from my face like rain
Inside my soul was dying,
As I sat with my head hanging down
I felt all I could do was sigh
Then I heard a beautiful sound
And lifted my head to the sky
It was a miracle to behold
For a spell I could not breathe,
Clouds were the color of gold
My teary eyes could not believe,
A figure was being made
The shape of a man in the clouds,
I lifted my arms and prayed
Then the man said aloud,
"Tell me why my precious child
Do you hang your head so low?
Why do you not smile?
Please just let me know.
For there is nothing that can dim the light
Which shines inside of you,
But to escape darkness you must fight
And the light your soul manifests will see you through,

My spirit lives in you
Just as my word lies in your heart,
Forsake you I would never do
That's why our love will never part,
So hold your head up high
For there is no need for desperation,
Just as time passes by
So does every sad situation,
The next time that you find
That with life you cannot cope,
Look in the sky for my special sign
A Rainbow Of Hope."

# What Will Tomorrow Bring

As I look into the crystal ball
All I see is a blur,
Will I stand or will I fall?
Who knows what is to occur?

Will I meet death face to face?
Will I rejoice or will I weep?
Will my world be nothing but empty space?
When I awaken from my sleep?

How will I know, what will I do?
Will situations be beyond my control?
Can this all be really true?
Will I have time to save my soul?

How do I know what tomorrow will bring?
Other than a brand new day,
Will I hear the bells of heaven ring?
Or will Hell take my spirit away?

As I close my eyes to go to bed
I ask the Most High my soul to keep,
I hear Gods voice inside my head
Have no fear, Just go to sleep,

No matter what happens to you tomorrow
Know that I will always be by your side,
Whether you experience joy or sorrow
My light will always be your guide.

# In These Trying Times

The smoke is so dense that one cannot see
The pain is so deep that one cannot tell,
I watch as the blood drips slowly off of me
The fire is burning in Hell,

The Devil works fast
The chosen will last
The weak will reap what they sow,
The time is near
My heart filled with fear
In the end God will know,

Why do I stand by
Why can I not fly
Can anyone tell me why,
Tears I cry
For living a lie
Where will I go when I die,

Why does the sun only shine in the day
Why do stars sparkle only at night,
In times like this, my mind starts to go astray
But it's these trying times when you hold me tight.

# One Day

One day I will be known for something special
I will be known for something good,
I will be known for beating the odds
When nobody thought I could,
One day,

One day when people say my name
They will say my name with respect,
My name will bring my family honor
A name that nobody can forget,
One day,

One day I will touch the hearts of every man and child
I will heal the sick and comfort the sad and blue,
I will give inspiration to carry on the struggle
And I won't stop until all this is true,
One day,

One day I will stand on top of the mountain
And look down at everything below,
I will give my Creator the highest praise
For allowing my light to glow,
One day,

One day I will see the Most High
And he will say my child, my son,
The world is a better place because of you
But on this day your work is done,
One day.

# Am I Yet A Man

I was talking with the Most High one night
It started as a normal conversation,
He said that I had been through a lot-
Many a trial and tribulation,

But through it all I had persevered
Many a lesson I had learned,
He had watched me grow throughout my years
And everything I achieved I earned,

Many mistakes I had made
Many wrong directions I took,
But then I finally saw the light
When to the source of my soul I did look,

Then I asked him one question,
For I still did not understand,
He said you followed my plan,
You took my hand,
And then you died a man

# The Kiss Of An Angel

I have had a kiss from an angel
That left me out of breath,
I have had a kiss from an angel
The angel of death,

The angel flew down
And kissed me goodnight,
The angel flew down
And then I saw the light,

# The Beginning Of The Never Ending

The Clock Struck NOW.
Symbolizing the beginning of the never ending,
representing phases of time,
spaces of rhyme that never connected.
Although they protected the sacred tribes
with the vibes of the fire,
so they danced in the wind
with the desire to defend what they held to be true.
But some had turned blue in the face
because they forgot how to breathe
and believe
in the grace of the clouds
and the rain.
So the pain was felt as the train began to melt the tracks,
therefore ending the same way back
from where they just left,
which was the breath they never took,
opening the book that never ends,
like the opposite of trends
that we believe to be our friends,
but fads die when souls fry,
because the sun's rays become so hot they burn,
but to many love to play in the flame,
so they place the blame on what they yearn to keep,
which is unfair.
So they will sleep in the caves
until they can behave like they can
Once they overstand the plan
that we must all figure out or perish.
So they cherish the core of the fire

which is the desire to ignite the torch
to watch the light scorch through the tundra
quenching its thirst at the Nile.


Meanwhile...
the whole wild scene was being seen by the jury,
and in a blind fury they dismissed the evidence
admitted by the state.
Recognizing nonsense in the lawyers' debate,
while unconsciously realizing the suspect's fate
was being sealed
by the lick of the dog upon the earth's cheek.
But they felt that rain brought the highest peak of pain.
So their brains never recovered
the secret treasure that is rarely discovered,
because mankind's mind must struggle to find reason.
As the fall of the winter brings a new season in time.
Symbolized by the chime of the bell.
So Hell kept on giving us the impression
that we were all living for the golden color of the candle,
which was really a scandal all in itself.
For the vandal was death
who placed the breath upon the shelf,
as if it were a left shoe
with no right home.
Like an extra-terrestial from celestial lands,
but one who fully overstands the power of love.
So the shower they shoved through the air
still did not share the fragile care that their hearts held,
because they failed at their sole goal,
which was regaining the light that shines in their soul,
but no one voted when the polls were open.
So lost souls kept on hoping

that one day their sacred scrolls
could rope in some type of champ.
So that when the lamp was lit it would forever burn.
But because they were forgetful
they could not remember what they had learned.
So they still burned at the stake
because of the moves they chose to make
when in a spiritual drought.
Sinking deeper and deeper into tunnels of doubt,
being saved only by the slave at the helm of Hades'
infamous River Styx.
Hey! These sticks hurt bones.
Though thick they stick to paper,
making a full caper out of what was to only to be an idea
suspended in time like a pause in the words I speak,
because the weak find they are truly strong
when they peek into their minds
realizing divine notions for real.
Just like oceans of steel,
still being as soft as the water
their waves crash against the land.
Undercurrents carrying back sand to the sea,
so that it now  has a home
deep inside of the dome,
a.k.a.,
the atmosphere.
Making it clear how minute
the guns we shoot are to our deaths,
which are only pauses of breath
from one zone to the next.
But  when wondering what is next
our thoughts become perplexed.
"Its To Complex," we yell and shout.

So we pout in the day and sleep at night.
Awaiting the sight of Time's midnight.
But once it comes,
we run to the sun of a new day,
becoming a game we all love to play
and we actually think we can win.
Starting the sin again even when it paused.
Restarted only because
when brokenhearted the soul has no control over emotions.
So will  political potions of tax
ever cure us of the facts that we trust to be pure
in the beginning of the never ending
drama.
Trauma experts are called to save the hurt slave
before the grave is reached
and security of the heaven's breached by the four star,
whose car is driven by a man said to be free,
but who has no free will.
So will the strange ever change like the history they tell,
or will the mystery of how to escape this living Hell
be forever kept in Hell,
where no blindman can see the true prophecy.
Detailing how we should all be sitting on thrones
and sleeping in zones with the spirits
LISTEN!!!
as they beg for you to hear it,
like the mark of the beast being implanted
MICROCHIPS
but many will take it for granted
as if  it's only another set of fingerprints
so situations will become tense as dense molecules
see themselves as fools swimming around in schools
with their eyes always watching

and ears catching the latest news,
while at the same time expressing views of disgust
about how spiritual rust has stagnated Mother Earth's crust,
which they want inhabited by human robots
who place materials before the imperial reason
in which we all come,
making the drums play no beat at all,
for human hands can only brace the fall,
Know that without feet no one can stand as tall
as the king cobra
as he dances to the tune of the sun and the moon,
soon to be our home as we roam forever,
BECAUSE IT NEVER ENDS
only begins in different dimensions
because of scientists Top Secret evil intentions,
we must disable them indeed,
and move with speed before the door is closed
like the petals of the rose who never left the bud,
Our souls were given a second chance with flesh and blood
yet some still insist on having an impure mentality
whose only reality is money green.
That's why the causality can now be seen on the big screen.
So screen what your brain thinks,
because your nose knows you say no because it stinks.
But you still drink as if in your last cup you are drowning
to look up at the frowning moon
as it was clowning its darker,
but other half,
but another's laugh can never laugh last,
so the paragraph never ends.
Because no man can begin to fathom the date
when the Creator had begun
to shape the sun and the universe as his first child,

Because the mind is too wild to be calm.
Causing the palm to lay upon my mother,
smothered in the blanket of the night before my brother,
who is always my kin in spirit and never in sin
is brought back to a house soon to be his home
only for a little bit.
How considerate can you get they wonder
as the thunder claps
the son slaps his mother,
awakening her from her nap
as she was sneaking between levels
deeper than any shovels could dig
out of the earth
whose birth
cannot even begin to explain
The Beginning of the Never Ending.

# Away In Dreamland

# Nubian Queen

When my eyes met yours, I felt a warm presence
A true Nubian Queen to behold in the essence,
At that moment, I knew you were unlike any other
A woman that deserves the utmost respect from a brother,
For you are a Queen, so you should be treated as such
You need to be desired for your intellect as well as your touch,
The gifts the Creator blessed you with are far beyond measure
The richness in your heart makes your soul a valued treasure,
You are an angel manifested into human form
Your perfected body is protected by the eye of every storm,
You have a mind that posesses the wisdom of the divine
Your heavenly body is a beautiful shrine,
Your voice sends subliminal messages everytime you speak
You stand tall through all adversity as others grow weak,
When my eyes met yours, I saw what I had never before seen
The breathtaking presence of a Nubian Queen.

# In The Air

When you and I breathe
I know that the air is not the same,
But it is that same air that separates us
That allows you to be with me at all times
For it is in the air that I hear your sweet harmonic voice
Whispering and singing in my ear all the day long
For it is in the air that I smell your fragrance
As the breeze floats under my nose
For it is in the air that I feel your touch
As you slip through my fingers
At my every attempt to hold you near
For it is in the air that I see visions of your heavenly body
In the form of divinely sculpted clouds as they pass overhead
Although it is true all this in the air I do find
Without the air you would still be with me
For it is you that is always on my mind

# What You Do To Me

Your touch is that of a cold winter's night
The sensation gives my body chills,
But warmth fills my body when I hold you tight
The powers you posses are surreal.

Not even candy gives me a sweeter taste
Then when your lips touch mine,
My heart beats fast when I feel your embrace
For your magic is truly divine.

I feel as if an enchanted spell I am under
By just the mere mention of your name,
Sometimes I do nothing but sit and wonder
If you too feel the same.

Your sweet voice is music to my ears
Caressing them with every word you speak,
Why then do you have my mind in fear
And my body feeling weak,

It is because I am scared of what I feel inside
I know deep in my soul this to be true,
But from you my feelings I will no longer hide
Because I have fallen in love with you

# My Mermaid

Where is my mermaid?
Oh where could she be,
Where is that special woman
Made just for me?

Although they say
There are many fish in the sea,
I know that only my mermaid
Is the perfect one for me,

I have searched every sea
From the Black to the Red,
But still no signs do I find
Of the one I'm to wed,

One day I will find her
This I know to be true,
But until then I'll keep looking
And sailing the ocean blue.

# Your Beauty

The world is replete of natural beauty,
A tranquil waterfall flowing into a shallow brook,
A colorful rainbow rising over the horizon at dawn,
Butterflies dancing playfully in the wind,
But to your beauty can none of these compare,
For beauty is personified in everything you do,
Every word that flows from your mouth
Is both sensual and enchanting,
Dazzling are your sparkling eyes as they
Twinkle like the stars in the sky above,
Your radiant smile illuminates the face of all who behold it,
Captivating is your physique as it is graceful in motion,
Your majestic persona epitomizes the word Goddess,
Yours is a beauty that will never fade or grow old
For yours is a rare beauty that transcends from your soul.

# On My Mind

As the sun beams down its marvelous rays
I watch as the hands of time pass me by,
In my heart your love forever stays
For you are the twinkle in my eye.

You are on my mind every minute of every day
From when I awaken until my day is through,
Before going to sleep I kneel down and pray
That I will have sweet dreams of you.

I think of your smile, I think of your touch
I think of all the fun things we have done,
These are the reasons I miss you so much
And why I know you are that special one,

So I pray everyday to the Lord up above
To bring my angel back to me,
For you are the only one I can ever love
And love you I will for all eternity.

# My Lucky Star

Pale is the moon, on this cold bitter night,
Alone I stand, without another  soul in sight,
There is nothing but darkness,
for as far as my tired eyes can see
I have lost my sense of direction, My sense of purpose,
My sense to be me,

I wish upon a star tonight
That a miracle fall from above
I wish upon a star tonight
To help me find true love

What is that light I see glowing from afar
I wonder if it could be my lucky star
It twinkles as if to communicate, Its light dancing as it shines
I wonder if I follow it, Could happiness once again be mine?

Could you be my lucky star?
Could you be my fantasy come true?
Or are you just a masquerade?
I have no clue of what to do

I have decided to take my chances,
I hope your guiding light leads the way
But if it is destiny that it does not,
I know I will  be no more lost than I am today,
With nothing to lose and everything to gain,
I embark on my heart's quest
With so much past heartache and pain,
 I hope that it has finally found a place to rest,

Could you be my lucky star?
Could you be my fantasy come true?
I have no idea of who you are
But your light I will pursue

Even though my eyes are opened wide,
I still do not believe what I see
It is a haven full of beauty and peace
Lying right in front of me,
My lucky star has led me to a place
Where I have forever longed to be
With the help of my star,
My fantasies and dreams are now reality,

I wish upon my lucky star
That you will forever stay by my side,
The twinkle in my eye you are
Just as you are my heart's guide

# When Queens Mourn

I looked deeply into your eyes
It was there I saw the source of your pain,
My temperature quickly began to rise
As I searched for ways to help you sustain,

For I have helplessly watched you suffer for so many years
I have seen the many ways your precious heart has been torn,
I wanted desperately to find a way to stop your tears
But nobody had told me what to do when Queens mourn,

How could I mend your broken heart?
How could I ever find the right words to say?
How could I stop your world from falling apart?
How could I show you a brighter day?

How could I rescue you from your living Hell?
How could I stop your children from slowly dying?
How could I pick up your pieces as they fell?
How could I stop your endless crying?

Then I heard a divine voice from up above
Telling me he had the situation under control,
He said when a Queen mourns all you must do is give her love
And the light will manifest in her soul,

So I looked back into your eyes
It was then I saw what had been there all along,
For the power and strength of your soul made me realize
Why through it all, you have always been so strong,

As a King I promise to always stand by your side
To hold and comfort you whenever you are concerned,
Now all we must do is let pure love be our guide
And for eternity our fire will burn.

# Away In Dreamland

As I close my eyes
I feel as if I am away in a beautiful land,
I can feel the water flowing under me
As I lay there on the sand,
The sound of the waves
Helps to put my restless mind at ease,
The air is crisp and clear
With only a slight hint of a breeze,
And there you are
As beautiful as the stars up above,
The only one my heart beats for
The only one my mind is forever thinking of,
As you lay there on the beach
With your body next to mine,
I feel so content at this moment
I wish I could stop the hands of time,
If only I could have you by my side
For the rest of my days,
But you are just part of a dream
That I know will soon fade away,
But as my eyes open
I realize that things aren't always what they seem,
For there you are beside me,
Oh, life is but a dream

# Out of the Darkness

# Tell Me My Story

Shadows and spirits that lurk in my mind
Whispering voices that speak to my soul,
Release me from these shackles that bind
Tell me my story, so that I may become whole,

Be my guiding light through all the masquerades
Leading me to a divine oasis where lies end and truth begins,
Bring me out of the darkness, for I am no longer afraid
Come now oh ancient spirits and tell me where I have been,

Tell me oh Nubian Kings and Queens
How you used to sit upon majestic thrones,
Drink the pure nectar  of the river Nile
And build ingenious temples of stone,

Tell me how you charted the heavenly stars in the sky
And danced all night with the rhythm of the drums,
Make my flesh tremble when it hears your mighty war cry
Tell me your ancient secrets so that I too may overcome,

Then tell me the pain of being shackled and chained
Drowning in the Atlantic and being herded like livestock,
Tell me how you used to constantly struggle and strain
But yet and still be sold at the auctioning block,

Tell me how it feels to be worked so hard
That your muscles begin to be ripped from your aching bones,
Tell me how it feels to see your mothers and daughters raped
And all you can do is beg your massa to leave them alone,

Tell me how it feels to have blood gushing from you back
To helplessly hang from a tree with dogs biting at your feet,
Tell me how it feels to be hated because your skin is black
Reveal to me the cowards that hide behind white sheets,

Tell me about fields replete with cotton and sugarcane
Looking out your window at night only to see a flaming cross,
Tell me all about your forgottten struggle and pain
Tell me how many millions of precious lives were lost,

Tell me about separate and unequal living conditions
Bus  boycotts and being locked inside of prison walls,
Tell me how you let nothing stop you from your mission
Show me where you found the strength to still stand tall,

Tell me about your children who have never seen their fathers
Public housing packed with pistols and welfare checks,
Tell me why many can help out, but so few ever bother
Tell me why Nubian Queens seldom receive their due respect,

Tell me about viruses that are killing off my sisters and brothers
Let me know how it feels to inhale crack through my lungs,
Tell me why Africa's beloved are aborted by their mothers
Tell me how we were robbed of our native tongues,

Oh, ancient spirits of ancestors past
Open your sacred doors and let me in,
Give me all the answers to the questions that I ask
But most of all tell me where I have been,

For it is only after I know where I come from
That I will have the wisdom to make it where I am headed,
I thank you for all that I am and all that I will ever become
For it is deep in my soul that your eternal flame is embedded,

Tell me my story
Oh ancient spirits
Tell me my story.

# I Ain't Gonna Study War No More

I ain't gonna study war no more
War ain't ne'er done me no good,
I ne'er knew what I was fighting for
I only fought cause I thought I should,

Mama always told me not to fight
It went in one ear and out the other,
She said look in your soul and see the light
Instead of trying to kill your own brother,

I should've listened to mama from the start
Now I'm dead and don't know what for,
Got beat up and stabbed right in the heart
Naw, I ain't gonna study war no more.

# There Ain't No Sunshine

There ain't no sunshine in the streets at night
As the souls of the bloody victims meet their maker,
There are no smiles, only faces of fright
When their eyes finally see the undertaker,

He wears no mask, only faces of death
Dressed in all black from head to toe,
People sometimes ask when they take their last breath
Why did he feel it was their time to go,

The undertaker replies with a hideous laugh
I am not the one who took the life out of your soul,
Your brother is the one who delivered this deadly wrath
So ask him why your body is now so cold,

There ain't no sunshine in the streets at night
As the war zone grows bigger and bigger,
Only black soldiers are allowed to fight
In the war to kill off the so called nigger,

There is only one rule that they follow in the field
Society embedded one thought in their head,
If they look like you, then shoot to kill
But never have remorse for the dead,

For they are animals just like you
With nothing but beast like instincts,
It is the only thing I have trained you to do
That is to help make your race extinct,

There ain't no sunshine in the streets at night
As mourning families kneel down on their knees to pray,
Lord please help the soldiers to see the light
Before they cause us all to see our last day.

# Forever Entrapped

I could hear the dogs barking as they yelled everyone's name,
"Boy, Boy!"
It only made us run faster.
Won't no way master was gonna catch us now.
Somehow we had to escape.
I am tired of getting raped and working for free.
I'm tired of them abusing me!
They said they got a path that will take us right to the coast of
Mexico.
"Come on y'all, we got to hurry up and go.
They say everybody can ship off down there.
That they don't care what kind of worker your barcode said you
wuz,
cuz they don't even got scanners like the new world does."

They continued to run.
Hiding in the shadows of the sun,
filled with hopes of finally becoming free,
and then they saw a divinely glowing object
hanging from a tree.

I had heard before that books were real,
but I never thought that my hands could feel the touch of one.
"Come here son. This is one of them things
your great granddaddy used to read.
He said his master used to make his fingers bleed
every time he got caught with one in his hand.
"But daddy, I don't understand.
What do those symbols mean that are painted on the walls
of those golden triangles?

I don't know, but we gotta go.
Cuz, the promised land is awaiting us!

They continued to run until they had snuck across the fences
leading into Mexico.

"Daddy, we finally made it. Let's go look for some real jobs.
There go somebody right there.
"Can we work for you sir?"
Me and my dad ain't worried about making rank.
We just tired of sleeping behind bars every night.
We wanna volunteer for an outer space flight
 to explore the new universe."
"Yeah, you boys look real strong
and you seem smarter than most,
There is a spaceship set to leave off the coast at dawn.
You're working for me now, so change your name
from boy to pawn."

They were just about to get on the ship to leave Hell and go to
the promised land when they heard,
"Boy, Boy.
Time to get back to work, and that's the last time I'm going to
tell y'all about using that virtual freedom machine during
break."

# When The Slugs Penetrate

As hard as I try I can never forget the terror
I felt on that grave night
My heart was pounding through my chest
as I held my covers tight,
The echo of the bullets rang in my ear
as they sliced through the dense air
I knew this night was different than all the others,
for reasons I am now aware,

The eerie feeling I had got worse
as the horror settled in the bottom of my soul
The sweat that was pouring out of my skin
left my drained body feeling cold,
Time and time again I ask myself
if I was meant to be that bullets destination
But I knew deep in my heart that I wasn't
as soon as I felt the slug's penetration,

I remember trying to call out to my parents,
begging them to come stop the pain
But blood was the only thing that came out of my mouth
as it ascended to my brain,
I can recall following a bright light
as it slowly guided me to the divine
He told me that I still had my whole life ahead of me
and that now was not my time,

When my eyes finally opened
I was surrounded by people dressed in white,
Then all the painful memories were brought back
of that dreadful January night,
I struggled and strained to sit up and look around,
but found myself unable to rise
The sadness I felt was immeasurable
when the doctor informed me I was paralyzed,

From the neck down I had lost all my nerves,
I could not even feel the slightest touch
I still wonder to this day how one stray bullet
could destroy my life so much,
It was on the night of my tenth birthday
when fate dealt me that terrible blow
I can still remember it like yesterday
although it happened twenty years ago,

The man who pulled the trigger served five years
and then they let him out on parole
I cannot bring myself to forgive him
although I truly want to deep in my soul,
I became living proof that bullets carry no name,
nor do they discriminate
This is my painful story of that horrid night
when I felt that crippling slug penetrate,

# The Attack

My eyes closed for the night
But I heard horrid voices in my head,
Instantly I was filled with fright
And all I could see was red,
Suddenly out of the mist
Appears this horrendous looking beast,
He looked at me and licked his fangs
As if I was to be his next feast
His hands took hold of my heart
And he demanded that I listen to what he had to say,
He told me he had a special game
That he wanted me to play,
His words sounded wicked and eerie
I could feel them trying to infiltrate my mind,
I could tell what he was saying
But his message was unrefined,
I could feel every ounce of his power
As he began to wage a war with my soul,
He was fighting hard to dominate my mind
He was dying to take control,
My thoughts were severely perplexed
As I contemplated his evil plan,
He wanted me to turn on my own people
By killing another man,

To his evil and vicious plot
I did nothing but refuse,
I know only the Devil would win that game
And everyone else would lose,
He said there was no way I could defy him
I looked him in his eyes and told him he was wrong
I told him there was no fear in my heart
For God always stands strong,
He became furious
And soon began to disappear,
He said one day he'd have my soul
And that I would forever live in fear,
Even though I had survived the battle
I knew that he would soon be back,
All he is doing is waiting for the right time
All he is doing is planning for his next attack.

# All I See Is Black

In the midst of the sweltering midday sun
All my eyes can see is black,
I try to stay strong and fight the pain
But the tears keep coming back,

My son died here a year ago
He was killed on this very date,
I watched in tears as he was hung
For trying to find an escape,

I feel as if I am trapped under a cloud
That is forever dropping rain,
Deep in my heart there is warmth and joy
But all I can feel is the pain,

A strong black woman I am
I pray there will be more strong after me,
Unfortunate I am to be a slave
I pray that they all be free.

# A Slave's Surprise

From the shallow confines of my grave
I am once again blessed with the gift of breath
For not to long ago I had died a slave
But I was given another chance after death

I thought the world would be a better place
Since the last time I had opened my eyes
But what I see now is nothing but a disgrace
I could not have dreamt of a worst surprise

Oh no, What have my children done?
After all we struggled to achieve
My mind is shocked and stunned
All of this madness I cannot believe

Black men are dying everywhere
Being killed by the hands of another
Are they unaware or just don't care
About the love they should have for each other

We fought hard for so many years
So that our children may be free
Now my children have made real my worst fears
As they kill each other, they also kill a part of me

Soon my people will be nothing but a memory
If all of the senseless bloodshed does not cease
With just a slight chance of that becoming reality
My soul will never be able to rest in peace.

# The Burning Fire Quenches My Thirst

The burning fire quenches my thirst
But the ashes leave me hungry for more,
My expanding mind is about to burst
As my thoughts take off and soar,

As the mirage of truth catches my eyes
A divine voice inside my soul tells me no,
Do not be deceived by a living lie
Look deeper and the truth will show,

I asked this  voice what do you mean
They could not have lied for all these years,
My son, only after the truth has been seen
Will you understand the reason for your tears,

So I begin my mission with good intent
To identify where my people have really been,
But all I can find is a lot of lament
Until the truth was revealed by God my friend,

What is the secret lying in that book
Why do you wish not to tell,
I open it wide and take a look
As I start a journey through Heaven and Hell,

As the tears start to burn my eyes
Anger and joy starts to fill my heart,
Why have they camouflauged the truth with lies
They should have been honest from the start,

For many years I have fought in vain
Now I understand the reason why,
For my people have experienced much heartache and pain
For the facts I am now ready to die,

Some will never know what lies in the past
Some will stay ignorant and blind,
As I journey through my story I know I will last
Because it is in the burning fire that the truth I find.

# Triple Three

As I waited for my turn to be scanned, I looked at the old man in front of me. I wondered why he never ran once he reached the other side. It was as if he wasn't scared of dying, like in his own mind he had already died.

They began calling out our names, "115-24-9308, 748-59-4348, 214-95-2333." That was me. "Here sir", I yelled, "I request permission to enter my home. I request permission to enter Hell. I never liked the things that they made us say, but that is the American way, and who ever had a choice in this land anyway. As always I secretly began to pray that I would live through the day and be able to see the beautiful light of the virtual sunrise machine tomorrow at school.

"Hurry up Triple Three. I don't suppose you want to hang from a tree like your ancestors," the humanoid said. I don't know why he said these sort of things, because he knew as well as I did there were no trees left after the wrath of the last civil war. One half of the world fighting against the other, brother against brother. They say it ain't gon ever be another war, but some say the aliens just waiting for the right time to attack. Some didn't even believe in aliens way back, but I guess the past is the past. I just gotta worry about making it to my cell. You can never tell these days, but I've almost mastered making it home without getting shot! All I do is picture my cot and the promised land, because my master told me one day I could stand on land that was really green, and that he had seen outside of the dome. The scanner read my barcode and I began the long way home.

I tried to not let the sound enter into my ears, but I could hear the blasts of the guns, as the sons shot at pictures of their fathers. I never bothered to join them, because sometimes they would get upset and end up shooting at each other. I saw the detour sign. Oh, how I hated to see the detour sign. I began to put on my gas mask and injected myself with the AIDS vaccination. It almost made me sick to have to walk through that nasty graveyard time after time again. It forced me to look at all those in my dome who had been killed with the disease. Their decayed bodies were stacked on top of each other, as if they were bales of hay. Some say they only make us walk through there to show us what they have the power to do to us if we dare to have a revolution.

I had finally made it to my cell block. It looked like most of my friends had already been put to sleep for the night, because I couldn't hear any of them crying. They must have worked them real hard in the water purification fields, because they never inject them with marijuana resin unless they really felt sorry for them. I always thought it was too bad that they couldn't go to school like me. After all, some of them only registered one or two shades darker than me on the scale. But we were all property of this world. We were all inhabitants of Hell. So I scanned myself into my cell, closed my eyes, and prayed that tonight the dream machine did not fail.

# Out of the Darkness

Out of the darkness I come
with the grave intensity
of a tribal warrior
in the heat of battle
I come
with the explosive force
of an erupting volcano
blasting molten lava
out of its mouth
I come
with the suspenseful tension of a nation
moments before the controversial verdict is read

Out of the darkness
I come

To resurrect the living dead

I come
with the spirit of the brave
with the courage of those Nubians
who would rather the Atlantic be their grave
than to be someone's slave
I come
because I can see the shackles
around their bones
as they lay  below the ocean's waves

Out of the darkness
I come
because late at night
I can hear the horrifying screams
that the prison guard cannot
as multitudes of young men
cry out
"Somebody Save Me,"
because they can feel death
being brutally thrust into their rectum
by way of the HIV virus

Out of the darkness
I come
because early in the morning
I can see the Devil
as he camouflages himself
in the form of little white rocks
burning with the gases of death,
as breaths of living Hell are inhaled
injecting women 7 months into their pregnancy
with lies of highs that only bring lows
constantly delivering blow after life shattering blow.
For their premature born baby
that will never have a chance to fully grow
Out of the darkness
I come
because I am tired of seeing the beautiful flesh
of Mother Africa
being overly exposed
to any and all of those who have eyes

Out of the darkness
I come
because in reality my eyes have never seen a whore
only a Queen that has been mislead somewhere down the line
Out of the darkness
I come
because my soul can feel the pain
of the grieving mother
as she screams out
"Not My Baby!"
as she comes to the realization that her child is gone forever
all because he happened
to be at the wrong place at the wrong time
I come
because the water that I drink
doesn't have pure taste
I come
because the air that I breathe
is filled with toxic waste
I come
because they sell lung cancer
in the form of an addictive stress reliever
I come
because they wanted something
that could make black men sterile
while at the same time make their mind and body sicker
I come
because racism invented malt liquor
I come
because I see the evil plot grow thicker
right before my very eyes

Out of the darkness
I come
swimming through oceans of tears
all those before me have cried
Out of the darkness
I come
appealing the verdicts
of all those who have been unfairly tried
Out of the darkness
I come
searching to find the truth
everywhere the media has lied
Out of the darkness
I come
because I am tired of the less fortunate
being cast aside
Out of the darkness
I come
to bring an end to suicide
I come
to bring an end to homicide
I come
to bring an end to genocide
Out of the darkness
I come
to touch every living soul worldwide
Out of the darkness
I come
with the strength of God on my side

Out of the darkness
I come
with enough love and light
to make the Devil himself run and hide
Out of the darkness
I come
to unite a people
who they have attempted to divide
Out of the darkness
I come
because it's past time for you to decide
Out of the darkness
I come
because its past time for you to decide
Out of the darkness
I come
to open the door
so that you too may step inside
Out of the darkness